Ed, smiles

old

Hsl.

SAY, UNCLE

A Completely Uncalled-for History of the U. S.

SAY, UNCLE

A Completely Uncalled-for History of the U. S.

by

ERIC NICOL & PETER WHALLEY

SAY, UNCLE

FIRST EDITION, 1961
FIRST CANADIAN EDITION, 1963
SECOND CANADIAN PRINTING, 1965

PRINTED AND BOUND IN CANADA
BY THE RYERSON PRESS, TORONTO

With apologies to Sellar and Yeatman,
the American Historical Association,
and anybody else
who feels bad about it.

SAY, UNCLE

A Completely Uncalled-for History of the U. S.

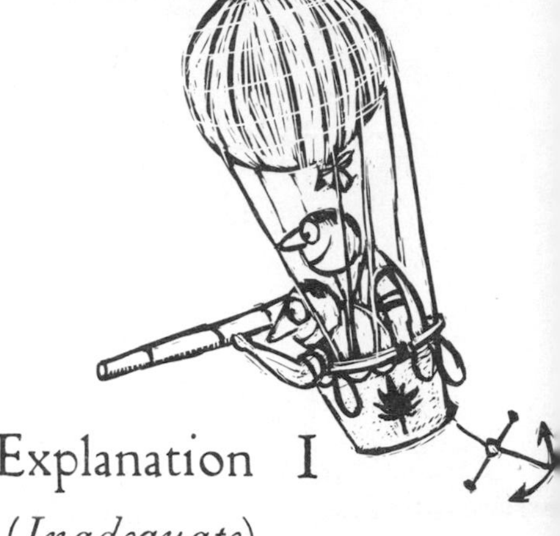

An Explanation I

(*Inadequate*)

A HISTORY OF THE UNITED STATES BY TWO CANADIANS who know nothing about the subject would seem to be, to say the least of it, unnecessary.

As you get into the book, however, you will perceive that what you had assumed to be a mild presumptuousness on the part of the authors was actually gross insolence.

There could indeed be no justification whatever for publication of the book were it not for the publisher's belief that Americans should see themselves as others see them (from below, and slightly to the left).

That is, American-written histories of the U.S., and those written by foreigners hoping to remain eligible for fellowships in that country, tend to treat certain figures as national heroes. About these historical characters a citizen of the British Commonwealth can be more objective. George Washington, for example, that troublemaker and traitor, we can put into proper perspective as a pretty nasty piece of goods who gave His Most Excellent Majesty, George III, a hard time.

Benedict Arnold, on the other hand, the authors see

as an enterprising chap who was entirely justified in what he did. We are confident that we would be doubly persuaded of this if we could remember what it was he did do.

The value of this approach to U.S. history will be immediately apparent to every thinking American. At a time when Americans are distressed by an unfriendly image of their country prevalent abroad, it can only be salutary to study what may be called the historical background to a spit in the eye.

The foreigner's ignorance that makes this work not only possible but invaluable has been greatly assisted by the unmanageable nature of American history.

For one thing, American history is more difficult to remember than British history because British history is marked off by monarchs, marching down time like ducks in a shooting gallery. It is a reasonably simple matter to remember that Charles II followed Charles I (sooner or later).* But there is no way of knowing whether President Jackson came before or after President Johnson, or if they were actually one and the same man.

U.S. history would have made a better impression among foreigners if Americans had elected their Presidents in alphabetical order. Instead, they got off on the

* He also followed Nell Gwyn, but that is another story. (Cf. Whalley and Nicol, *The Romance of the Orange,* Pippin Press, 1958.)

wrong foot with President Washington. And with John Adams right under their nose.

Aside from these natural aids to confusion the authors make acknowledgment to nobody else for the material in this book. Privately we admit that we haven't even been much help to each other.

To be absolutely frank, Whalley and Nicol didn't write the book at all. It was ghosted by Zsa Zsa Gabor.

W. & N.

II Prehistoric America (*Before Lawrence Welk*)

IN THE BEGINNING, THE WHOLE OF THE UNITED STATES was under water, except Milwaukee, which was under beer.

Proof of this is that Midwest farmers in ploughing have turned up clamshells, some millions of years old, others marked SOUVENIR OF LAGUNA BEACH.

The rich oil deposits of the central plains were built up by trillions of shrimps.* But over the eons the great plains became dry. (See chapter on Anti-Saloon League.) Some parts, such as Death Valley, rather overdid it. But most of the U.S. was a desirable prestige subdivision of North America, extending from Montezuma in the south to Minnehaha in the north.

The earliest residents of the United States, after the great lizards whose descendants may still be seen on the desert servicing slot machines, were the Indians.

The Indians were broken down into tribes. Some tribes were more broken-down than others, depending on how often they had been scalped by neighboring tribes.

* In Texas, prawns.

Life Among the American Indians (after an old print)

Say, Uncle

Famous American tribes of Indians include the Blackfeet, the Sioux, the Cleveland, and the Wooden. The Cleveland Indians were the ones that used finger language for words like "run," "walk," and "steal second."

The Indians' favorite method of attack was to come over a hill and pause outlined against the sky, then charge down and circle the enemy, riding single-file and pitching off their horses in droves.

Thanks to this method of warfare the Indians earned the title The Vanishing American. Their greatest contribution to American civilization was the custom of talking to each other by means of smoke, a method still used in hotel rooms at U.S. political conventions. (See "Politics, Indoor.")

America Discovered III

THE DISCOVERY OF AMERICA WAS AN ACCIDENT, FORTUnately not serious.

Christopher Columbus had been commissioned, among other things, by the Queen of Portugal, to help him find a new route to India.* Having no sense of direction but plenty of moxie, Columbus sailed west in his three ships, the *Santa María, Santa Lucia,* and *Santa Sees You.*

Contrary to popular belief, Columbus did not land up in Ohio. Instead he sailed full tilt into a group of islands off Florida. America was actually discovered in Flagrante Delicto, a beautiful island today owned by Ernest Hemingway.

Columbus found the natives of the islands very friendly, eager to give him anything he desired, so he called them the Virgin Islands, or West Undies. He took a pair of natives back to the Queen of Portugal, because she was crazy about novelty earrings.

"Here are two natives of India, or Indians," Columbus told the Queen.

* The Queen wanted more spice, the King being dead.

Columbus Sights the First Indian

"In a pig's valise they're Indians," said the Queen, who was knowledgeable. "Indians wear a white thing slung between their legs and have chutney on their breath."

Columbus was therefore recommissioned to find a new route to India and no goofing around this time. Columbus thereupon sailed west again and landed up among the same islands as before. This time the natives were not as eager to give him everything he wanted, so Columbus decided to call it America.

Returning to Portugal he told the Queen: "I've discovered America, your Majesty, and here to prove it is a heap of gold, popcorn and chewing gum."

"Pepper!" yelled the Queen. "Pepper is what you were sent for, and the poppies of Cathay."

Columbus hastily assembled another crew and set sail for India. When those same islands came into view, with the natives wearily waving at him to get lost, Columbus did not have the heart to go home and tell the Queen. However, by a stroke of good luck, he then died.

Columbus Lands in America

The Early Colonists (*Too Early*) IV

THE QUEEN OF PORTUGAL DID NOT TRY TO HOLD THE continent that Columbus had discovered, even as an investment. Other nations therefore dispatched explorers in a very close race, the Spaniards landing where they could take gold, the French landing where they could take furs, and the British landing where they could take the Spaniards and the French. (Also known as Union Jack.)

As a sideline the French also discovered New Orleans. At that time there was no jazz in New Orleans because the French were still Vieux Carrés, or Old Squares.

A Packet of Pilgrims V

VARIOUS COUNTRIES SENT COLONISTS TO AMERICA, BUT the English were the only ones that took it seriously.

This was because they were Pilgrims. At that time England had fallen under the influence of Charles II, who had spent some time in Paris, resulting in the persecution of everybody who didn't believe in living it up.

The Pilgrims' ship, the *Mayflower,* landed in the New World at Plymouth Rock, because it looked like the best place to be utterly miserable.

Pilgrims on Their Way to Church (after Boughton)

Almost immediately the Indians introduced the Pilgrims to the turkey and Indian corn, while the Pilgrims introduced the Indians to grapeshot and Christianity.

The first settlements of New England were frugal in the extreme. Everybody ate nothing but Boston baked beans, and there wasn't much social life apart from the Saturday-night drowning of a witch.

A Salem Witch Hunt

Life was simple. All the men were called John, all the women were called Mary, and practically everything was a sin but hard work. This work consisted in the main of constructing the most uncomfortable furniture imaginable, a craft honored to this day by the waiting rooms of U.S. airports.

Pleasure seekers were put in stocks. Backsliders were put in bonds. In fact so many sinners went into stocks and bonds that it was necessary to found the New York Stock Exchange.

This in turn required the purchase of New York from the Dutch colonists, who had called it New Amsterdam and were pretty fed up with trying to cut canals through the solid rock.

Say, Uncle

The Puritan settlers got Manhattan for a song ("Rock of Ages"). This was the beginning of the New Englander's reputation as a sharp trader, always looking for the Maine chance.

A Charming Tale, if True VI

AT THIS TIME A RATHER CHARMING EPISODE OCCURRED between Captain John Smith and a dusky Indian maiden named Pocahontas. In love with Pocahontas, a bashful friend of Captain Smith's begged Smith to ask Pocahontas if she would marry him (the friend). When Captain Smith did so, Pocahontas blushed prettily and said, "Speak for yourself, John." John did, and this was how he lost a friend but gained a squaw.

It also established a principle of American commerce: the middleman gets the gravy.

This romantic interlude is so famous in American history that, to this day, when loving couples register at a hotel, the gentleman signs them in as "Mr. and Mrs. John Smith." It is one of America's most honored traditions.

Pay Later

VII King George's Oversight

BEFORE LONG, THANKS TO THIS BOLDER APPROACH TO SEX, there were thirteen colonies instead of one.

During this important period the King of England was George III. American history has pictured George III as a big fat dummy. This description is not accurate. George III was a big fat dummy *who spoke German.* This is why he didn't realize that having thirteen colonies in America was unlucky. Also, names like Massachusetts made him sneeze.

George III therefore turned his face toward the Continent of Europe, where he would have a better chance of understanding somebody who called him a dirty name.

He was still facing the wrong way when the American colonists grew restive. In particular the colonists resented paying taxes to England. They thought that they should get something in return for the tax money, an attitude that shocked the English government and convinced the King that they had been brainwashed by the Redskins.

The colonial unrest reached its peak when a shipload of tea arrived in Boston harbor, and the thirsty Bostonians learned that the English had increased the levy. (Cf. old Anglo-American folk ballad, "I Been Workin' on the Levy.")

Incensed and largely Irish anyhow, the people of Boston tossed the teabags overboard and swore that they would get even with the English by learning to make decent coffee.

This incident resulted in formation of the Boston Tea Party, a political group dedicated to firing on undefended forts.

Arrival of the German Immigrants

VIII The American Revolution

(17? to ?83)

Nobody knows when the American Revolution started. The rebels were so badly organized that they forgot to make a note of the date, as well as having no shoes to speak of.

The first seeds of revolt were sowed by a group of hotheads, all named Adam—Samuel Adam, John Adam, Mary Adam, and so on. These people were especially upset about the Stamp Act, a British act which made it compulsory to buy stamps even though there was no postal service.

They therefore asked Benjamin Franklin to put down that blasted kite for a minute and print the Declaration of Natural Rights, according to which the colonies would have the right to be perfectly natural and no more of those fool wigs the English wore.

They also called the first Continental Congress, which voted unanimously to inform the British government that America was a continent and therefore too big to be pushed around.

The British government refused to take this seriously, being under the influence of the beginning of the Romantic Movement (absence makes the heart grow fonder). Instead Parliament passed the Maritime Act, according to which the whole of America was officially under water—except, of course, Milwaukee—and therefore under the British Navy.

This touched off bloodshed. For the occasion, Benjamin Franklin invented gunpowder.

The first American troops were the Minute Men. (Just add water and stir into an open revolt.) The Man of the Hour was George Washington. There were sixty Minute Men to every Man of the Hour.

These small, mobile forces confused the British, who were accustomed to marching against the enemy in a straight red line, even numbers being shot, odd numbers stepping up.

Yet at first the revolutionary army bogged down, owing to lack of equipment, bad luck, and snow that fell only on the American side of the battlefield.

Difficulties in Conducting the Revolutionary War

Moreover, their Esprit de Corps—a French unit that joined up because of the war in Canada—was always high. Too much wine. Then General Washington impressed his troops by throwing a dollar across the Potomac. Money went farther in those days.

The first American patriot of the war was Paul Revere, who left his regular job of making copper-bottomed pots to jump on his horse and ride through the countryside shouting, "The British are coming!"

Since he always did this at midnight people got pretty fed up with it. But one night he was right, the British *were* coming. For this he was made a hero, there being no other nominations.

Later, at the height of a British bombardment of one of their own forts, Betsy Ross made the first American flag. She did this by the rocket's red glare, and by hand. She also gave birth to the Daughters of the American Revolution.

While they were waiting for the British to make one of the gallant blunders for which General Gargoyle was famous, the revolutionary leaders drew up the Declaration of Independence. The author of this historic document was Thomas Jefferson, today generally recognized as being the brains behind the whole caper.

Disheartened by the Declaration of Independence (the British troops wanted life, liberty, and the pursuit of happiness just as much as anybody else and maybe more), as well as defeated by the French Navy that had sneaked into the war in violation of the Maritime Act, Cornwallis surrendered. Cornwallis was (a) a fort, (b) a general, (c) an Indian soup. (Do not mark more than three.)

IX Washington's Rise to Oblivion

INFORMED THAT BRITAIN HAD LOST HER AMERICAN COLONIES forever, George III became George IV. But it was too late.

The United States were already busy with their first act of independence, which was to have a depression. During this difficult period the man who held the new nation together was George Washington.

George Washington as a little boy was asked by his father who had chopped down the cherry tree. George said, "I cannot tell a lie. I did." Since that day, no American politician has ever lied, about chopping down a cherry tree.

Washington was elected the first President of the United States not only because he had won the War of Independence but because his profile was right for the first one-dollar bill.

Being elected President was bad for Washington's career, which had been promising. He seemed to have found his own level. Martha did very well with her chocolate business, but George became less and less active, especially after his death.

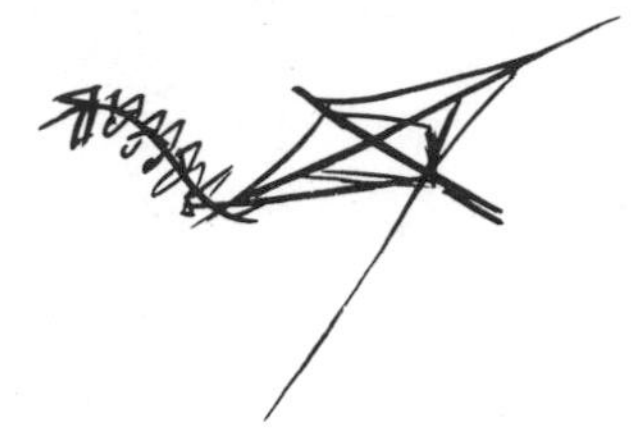

The First Americans X

ONCE THEY HAD WON THE RIGHT TO LIFE, LIBERTY, AND the pursuit of happiness, Americans went after what they really wanted: money.

Showing the way was the most enterprising of the new Americans, Benjamin Franklin. Franklin instituted Yankee ingenuity, which consisted of refusing to admit that anything was impossible except his wife.

Franklin invented everything, including lightning. He invented the Franklin stove, the Franklin automobile, a special cracked bell for British clocks (Big Ben), the alarm clock (Little Ben), and he made possible the first American newspaper by inventing the funnies (Uncle Ben).

Poor Richard

Say, Uncle

Franklin made bifocal glasses for people with split-level eyeballs. By this time he was so well loved by everybody that he was able to invent the harmonica.

The final thing Franklin invented was the Constitution, which he wrote, printed, and delivered on a bicycle of his own invention.

Benjamin Franklin gave future generations of Americans their best example of what can be achieved by hard work and thrift, but they don't hold it against him.

The Interbellum, or Dull, Period XI

After the War of Independence the United States stood around rather aimlessly, wondering what to do next. It was too early to open up the West and too late to practice Puritanism, burn witches, etc.

Some Americans wanted to march up and liberate Canada from the British, but other Americans had heard about the roads up there.

Instead, the American admiral John Paul Perry became a hero when he found that by sailing around the Great Lakes he could avoid the British Navy entirely.

His ship was called *Old Ironsides,* being made of wood, and later returned to Chicago to be converted into a seafood restaurant. Perry also led the first naval expedition to Japan, resulting in the opening up of Madame Butterfly.

To the south, a new territory was added to the thirteen colonies when King Louis, who owned Louisiana, found that he needed money, his wife having told the French peasants to eat cake and charge it.

The U.S.A. was therefore able to buy Louisiana from

Louis for a ridiculous figure. This history of being bought instead of fought over gave Louisiana an inferiority complex that led to the Kingfish, Amos 'n' Andy, and the illegitimate birth of the Blues.

American Invasion of Canada

The War of 1812, '13, etc. XII

VERY LITTLE IS KNOWN ABOUT THE WAR OF 1812 BEcause the Americans lost it.

It was one of the least popular wars the States has ever waged. It seemed like a good idea at the time (1812), because England and Napoleon had just opened in a war that promised to have a long run.

But the U.S. expeditionary force sent to liberate Canada found that the Canadians could march backward even faster than they could march forward. Retreat was their strongest weapon. They finally retreated the Americans right into the ground.

The United States has never tried to conquer Canada since. It knows that is worse than trying to eat peas with a knife.

Annoyed with the U.S. for taking advantage of the war with France, England not only defeated Napoleon but burned down Washington, D.C., which was only partly covered by insurance.

After rebuilding Washington the Americans decided to make it illegal for the capital of the United States to be burned down by foreigners. Congress therefore passed the Monroe Doctrine, named after a famous U.S. President (Andrew Jackson).

The Monroe Doctrine remains to this day the envy of all other countries, who wish that they had thought of it first. (Canada was allowed to share the same hemisphere as the United States for geographical reasons.)

The Monroe Doctrine

The Industrial Revolution XIII

(*rpm*)

WITH NO WARS TO DISTRACT THEM, THE AMERICANS BEgan producing things to make life easier. First of these was Eli Whitney's cotton gin, a device for making gin out of cotton. This machine was later replaced by the bathtub. (See "Twenties, Roaring.")

Next a prominent fishmonger named Robert Fulton piloted the first steamboat up the Hudson, ending the Age of Sail and adding a minstrel troupe that soon became famous as Fulton's Follies.

These paddlewheelers were the main river traffic, especially on the Mississippi, and helped to open up New Orleans, which has been wide open ever since.

Most famous of the Mississippi steamboats was the *Samuel Clemens,* because it was steered by Mark Twain, whose real name was Huckleberry Flynn.

But the most important American development in this part of the nineteenth century was that of the Iron Horse. The remarkable thing about the Iron Horse was that it was the first horse that ran on tracks and the tracks lost money.

Soon the American railroad had penetrated far enough west to be shot at by Indians. Flaming arrows turned dining-car passengers into short-order shish kebabs. And the trains were frequently held up by bandits, who divested everybody of their valuables. To this day, American train conductors keep taking out their watch to make sure they've still got it.

The Great Train Robbery

The Mexican War, Won by Davy Crockett

XIV

THE DEVELOPMENT OF THE RAILROAD WAS COUPLED WITH a growing realization that the United States had only one coast—the East. Men of vision saw that the U.S. would need more coasts for all the people, to leave room on the East Coast for all the money.

The upshot was the Mexican War, which started in an interesting way. An American citizen visiting a town in Texas entered a Mexican café and ordered a cup of coffee and a piece of apple pie with ice cream. The counterman brought the coffee and the pie, but no ice cream.

"You forgot the ice cream," complained the American. "I want apple pie à la mode."

Emotionally disturbed, the Mexican stabbed the American. When Washington (D.C.) heard about the incident, a troop of Texas Rangers were dispatched to drive the Mexicans out of the café and, while they were there, out of Texas. This the Rangers did by yelling:

"Remember the à la mode!"

Say, Uncle

The Mexican version of the Mexican War is somewhat different. According to the Mexicans the whole original idea of having a war was theirs, and the Americans got into the war only thanks to the generosity of Mexico's fat hero, Pauncho Villa. Villa was known as the first democratic Mexican because he would shoot at anybody regardless of race, creed, or color.

In any event Texas was thereafter called the Lone Star State, nobody wanting to be seen with the sheriff.

The California Gold Rush

Forty-Niners vs. Spanish Priests XV

THE TAKING OF TEXAS CLEARED THE WAY FOR THE FIRST gold rush to California, which till this time had been lying under a layer of Spanish missions.

The gold rush changed the entire tone of California. Enough money changed hands for the rough-and-ready miners to import wickedness, from Europe.

In addition to the European corn borer and grand opera, this wickedness brought women. Up till then a woman had been a voluminous buttress behind which a man could take shelter during an Indian attack.

The gold rush initiated new uses for women, such as separating the gold from the miner. This process took place in dancehalls and saloons where the girls flounced about. (Gold was worth $50 a flounce.)

The New England Quakers thus gave way to the San Francisco Quakers, a sect that believed in having a good time between shakes.

Those who failed to reach the coast settled for the next best thing, the great Salt Lake, where they became Mormons because they were unsinkable and therefore better than the Baptists.

XVI Legends of the Old West, Mostly Fibs

For those who failed to find gold the West offered other minerals in abundance. Lead, for example, could be picked up by anybody who cared to take a sample of Wyatt Earp.

Civilizing the West

Legends of the Old West, Mostly Fibs

The Old West was America's age of chivalry, when a man prized his honor above all other possessions, except his horse, which was usually his only other possession.

Cattle raising and sheepherding were popular hobbies among the frontiersmen, but the main occupation was practicing to be the Fastest Gun in the West.

One reason this trade was so popular was that it had a short apprenticeship. A top-drawer gunman spent most of the year traveling, at the invitation of the last town he was in, and was so popular that whenever he appeared in public he received a round.

Those cowboys who chose other professions—drinking, gambling, whittling, etc.—had to be very nimble to dive under tables during a shootout, or leap over bars, through windows and into horse troughs, thus qualifying as the first American pedestrians.

The hero of the Old West was notable not only for the variety of his adventures but also for the fact that each of them took 29 minutes 40 seconds, including commercials.

Most celebrated of the western desperadoes was Jesse James, who had a less distinguished brother, William, who was also known in England as Henry James. Between them the James boys pretty well covered the lively arts, though some of the credit goes to Whistler's Mother (Grandma Moses).

Brinkmanship

Legends of the Old West, Mostly Fibs

XVII Sitting Bull vs. Custard

GENERAL (LATER COLONEL) CUSTARD WAS A CRACK SHOT who could shoot a bird through the eye and was therefore called Bird's-eye Custard.

Despite previous military experience General Custard led his troop of soldiers into a trap laid by Chief Sitting Bull and his son Standing Calf.

Bravely, Colonel (later Sergeant) Custard refused to entertain the idea of surrender, which was just as well since Sitting Bull hadn't asked him.

The result was the Battle of the Little Big Horn, a river whose name didn't help matters. Of Sergeant (later Private) Custard's gallant regiment there were no survivors, other than several hundred artists who painted the scene and sold the pictures to school boards across the country.

Why the Indians Gave Up XVIII

SITTING BULL WAS IN TURN DEFEATED, AND MADE TO stand up, by the great American scout Buffalo Bill, with whom he exchanged shots till they were both pretty drunk.

This incident marked the beginning of the decline of the American Indian as we know him today. Most of the tribes filed glumly into government reservations

Geronimo Exiled to Florida

chosen because of a gummy, black stuff oozing out of the ground. The rest joined the circus.

Occasionally the Indians went on the warpath after drinking firewater—the water from old firebuckets. But by this time the U.S. Cavalry had learned how to arrive practically anywhere in the country at the eleventh hour (Mountain Time). Gradually the Indians accepted the spread of the white man's civilization, particularly the machine gun.

Old Black Joe and Other Problems XIX

The United States was thus able to turn its attention from its red-skinned people to its black-skinned people. Unbeknown to anybody, the Southern states had been importing colored people from Africa without a license.

These Africans became slaves on the Southern plantations, all the women being called Mammy and all the men Old Black Joe. Little ones were called pickin' ninnies because they picked less cotton than their elders.

The black slaves were happy, as slaves go, but they didn't go far. Runaway slaves were brought back and severely reprimanded, sometimes fatally.

But having slaves to do the work enabled the South to develop Gracious Living, the one thing that Benjamin Franklin hadn't thought of.

Gracious Living in the Old South consisted of waltzing for the young people and mint juleps for the elders, except when they were all on horseback, which was most of the time.

Say, Uncle

Just as Gracious Living was at its height, however, a writer named Harriet Beatty Stove wrote a book called *Uncle Tom's Cabin* which was inflammable.

This story was about an old slave (Uncle Tom) who couldn't pay the mortgage on his cabin and to avoid losing the place he had to put his daughter (Little Eva) on waivers, so that she was about to be picked up by a whip snapper (Sam McGee) when she was rescued by a friend of the family (Liza Doolittle), who was chased by bloodhounds (Ramblin' Rex and Georgia Tex) across the river ice till obliged to hand over the child to the angels, who pulled her up to heaven with block and tackle.

Uncle Tom's Cabin became a bestseller because it had been years since people had had a good cry. However, some persons reading between the lines—which was much harder in those days—saw the book as a dig at slavery.

These persons became so worked up that they drew a line between the North and the South, called it the Made-in-Dixie Line, and declared that everybody south of the line was a pill.

Lincoln and the Abortionists XX

INDIGNANT, THE SOUTH CALLED THOSE WHO WANTED TO do away with slavery Abortionists. But this did not bother the President, Abe Lincoln, who had been born in Illinois and was used to that kind of language.

Born in a log cabin, no other accommodation being available, Lincoln spent his early years being humble.

Good Evening, Abe

Lincoln worked as a rail splitter till he had enough planks to make a speaker's platform. He also studied law at night, so that he grew up homely.

By the time he was a young man Honest Abe, as he called himself, could argue that black was white. This won him the support of the Abortionists.

Lincoln had a very good sense of humor, but in those days the voters didn't hold it against you. He had a dry wit. He didn't drink, smoke, or run after women. He had no vices outside of politics.

Lincoln was not born with a silver spoon in his mouth but with something better: a golden tongue. He took on as many as three or four orators at a time, talking them into a heap. He was head and shoulders above other candidates, but just to make sure he wore a stovepipe hat.

The Civil War, an Unfortunate Occurrence XXI

THE MOMENT LINCOLN WAS ELECTED THE SOUTHERN states knew that they were in trouble. Lincoln could not waltz and had no experience with Gracious Living or any of the things people did who didn't have warts on their face.

To make the situation worse, the Abortionists were scrawling provocations on walls and buildings (Yankee doodles), and *Uncle Tom's Cabin* was outselling *The Racing Form.*

Matters were brought to a head with the finding of John Brown's body, a colored man who had been improperly buried and lay a-mouldering in his grave. When Lincoln complained about this, Virginia resigned from the Union and threatened to smoke all her tobacco herself. Hams, too.

Virginia was followed by all the other Southern states, who elected their own President, Jefferson Thomas. At school Jefferson had been voted the boy most likely to secede.

The Confederacy also issued its own money so that they wouldn't have to look at Lincoln on the two-dollar bill. Finally, the Confederates fired on Fort Sumptuous, the nicest fort the North had.

Lincoln was thus posed the problem of whether or not to set brother against brother, and sister against sister. (Mother and father had already been at each other for some time.)

The President decided to preserve the Union, and to make sure he was doing the right thing he signed the official Proclamation of Emasculation, which made all men free regardless of sex, color, or both.

Meantime there had been four or five years of battles going on all over the South, both in the Deep South and at the shallow end.

Most of the battles were won by the South's general, Robert E. Lee. The North's generals had more men but no middle initial.

Lee was especially good at defeating the Yankees at Bull Run. On horseback he was a commanding figure. The Union generals also looked like part of the horse, but it was the wrong part, thus failing to inspire the infantry.

Then Lee made the mistake of having a battle someplace other than Bull Run. He changed to Gettysburg, though he did not know his way around Gettysburg and Lincoln had Gettysburg's address.

Lincoln at Gettysburg

Lee's defeat opened the way for Sherman and his tanks to go marching through Georgia, unfairly eating regularly, after the South had run out of food owing to the famous Southern hospitality.

To prove how ungracious the North could be, Sherman set fire to Atlanta. The rebels then knew that they were fighting a foe that was beneath their dignity, and Lee surrendered victoriously at Appotonicknacks.

After the war was over, it was revealed that the real source of the conflict was that the North was mainly a manufacturing region while the South was mainly agricultural. *Uncle Tom's Cabin* collapsed at the news.

XXII Lincoln's Mistake

WITH THE CIVIL WAR OVER, PRESIDENT LINCOLN decided to relax by taking in a show. This was a mistake.

One of the actors at the theatre, John Wilkes Booth, always became insanely jealous if anybody else got the spotlight. So when Lincoln stepped into the presidential box, and everybody applauded, Booth pulled out a revolver and ad-libbed several bullets at the President.

Lincoln insisted on remaining in his seat till the intermission, to avoid disturbing people in the same row. When he was finally carried out he was found to be deceased. Since that time, no American President has been a patron of the theatre.

John Wilkes Booth was pursued into the neighboring countryside, where he took refuge in a barn. His impersonation of a cow was so convincing that the police had to burn the barn down to be sure they didn't arrest the wrong party. (This event marked the beginning of barn theatres in the East.)

Reconstruction, Also Known as Rockefeller XXIII

For twenty years after the assassination of Lincoln the United States had no history whatever. Nobody knows what the Americans were doing during this period, except that by 1890 the population had doubled.

Some of this increase was due to immigration. Irishmen who had immigrated during the potato famine were betrayed by one of their number (Patrick Henry)

Era of Reconstruction

when he mentioned meat in his letter to the Old Country. A great wave of Irish resulted from this blunder, along with similar waves of Italians, Armenians, and Poles, and enough Scotsmen to handle their money for them.

One reason for the general absence of activity was the development of photography. Whole families were kept immobilized for extended periods while photographers fiddled about under their hoods. Birdie watching took great chunks out of the working day, and some members of families—particularly uncles who drank—never re-

Bell Discovers the Telephone

covered the power of movement after being photographed.

In a desperate attempt to recapture some of the color of Abraham Lincoln, President James A. Garfield managed to be assassinated, but he still failed to catch on.

Introduction of Silver into the Economy–1895

XXIV The Spanish-American Waltz

THE ONLY PROJECT WORTH MENTIONING DURING THIS period was America's liberation of Cuba from Spain, which nobody liked much because of its bullfights and royalty that didn't do anything except lie around bleeding easily.

The American forces were led by Teddy Roosevelt, who rode at a full gallop up San Juan Hill shouting, "Damn the torpedoes! Full speed ahead!"

This so confused the Spaniards that they surrendered without firing a shot. Cuba has been liberated several times since, but none of the liberators has proved as popular with the United States as Roosevelt because he shaved regularly.

Teddy's foreign policy he described in his famous saying: "Speak softly and carry a big staff." This was the beginning of American bureaucracy as we know it today.

The Gay Nighties XXV

THE LAST DECADE OF THE CENTURY (WHICH CENTURY need not concern us here) was called the Gay Nighties, because women gave up the crinolines that had been causing them to roll out of bed (see "Revolution, Feminine"), and started wearing something more sociable.

Later these girls were called Bloomer Girls, Gibson Girls and the Girls That Married Dear Old Dad. The reason for this sudden emphasis on girls was that they appeared with tiny waists and large bustles, removing all remaining doubt that they were different from boys.

This pretty well finished the horse. The invention of the automobile didn't help any either. By the turn of the century women were firmly established as being almost as enjoyable as a good cigar. It was too early for the full acceptance of women as equals of men, but this was the thin edge of the wench.

XXVI War! (*Again?*)

THE UNITED STATES PLUNGED INTO WORLD WAR ONE, which was running in competition with the Ziegfeld Follies. The American soldiers were called Doughboys because they rose to the occasion.

On landing in France the troops cried, "La Fayette, we are here!" There was considerable disappointment when it was found that La Fayette was a male, and dead at that.

In this war the British introduced the tank, the Germans introduced poison gas, and the Americans introduced ice cream. The latter weapon proved irresistible, particularly with the civilians.

Also the United States Air Force, which had received a nice boost from the invention of the airplane by the

Wright Brothers, took an active part in the war as the Dawn Patrol. The war was nearly over before somebody thought to ask why they were getting up so early. The tradition has been maintained to this day by U.S. airlines, which always serve dinner at 5 A.M.

Wilson, the Funny President XXVII

THE GREAT WAR WAS CALLED "THE WAR TO END WAR" and it was not over before there broke out several wars to end the war to end war.

Realizing that this could go on forever, and cost the U.S. a lot of money and precious ice cream, President Wilson founded the League of Nations. Wilson was called an idealist because he wore a pince-nez and looked as if his feet hurt.

At the last minute, however, the United States decided not to join the League of Nations, having learned on good authority that it was full of foreigners. Wilson was carried off by an acute spasm of disgust, and leadership of the country fell to more practical men (Al Capone, Chester Conklin, and the Smith Brothers).

XXVIII The Roaring Twenties and Other Plumbing

ONE EFFECT OF THE WAR WAS A NEW STATUS OF FEMALES, who had torn up their petticoats for bandages, regardless of whether somebody was hurt or not.

This change was known as the Emaciation of Women. Starting at New Year's Eve, 1919, women became much slimmer, bobbed their hair, smoked cigarettes from long holders and spent their waking hours dancing the Charleston.

The next ten years were called the Roaring Twenties because everybody was making bathtub gin, and the mash made for noisy drains.

Prohibition

Another result of Prohibition, which had been voted for while all the drinking men were overseas and unable to defend themselves, was the rise of bootleggers and gangsters such as the notorious Capone, Dutch Schultz, and Renta Hertz.

Chicago's brief claim to the title of musical capital of the country was dashed when it was found that the violin cases people were carrying contained either hooch or machine guns.

The most notable incident of the gang wars was the St. Valentine's Day massacre, in which one mob lined another mob against a wall, and three Cupids shot them all through the heart with sawed-off bows and arrows.

The U.S. was so noisy during the decade, what with gin gurgling and gangs gunning and girls giggling, that nobody could even hear himself think. President Coolidge was one of the first to give up trying. "I do not choose to run," he said, and thus became the first lame-duck President.

Adding to the uproar, the mayor of New York was Johnny Walker, the popular distiller. Mayor Walker was responsible for the first serious, organized effort to keep boys off the street—speakeasies. Entrance to these clubs was by invitation only, to keep out the undesirable element, such as mothers from the Midwest looking for their daughters, police, and Indians on horseback.

With so much going on at home America had little

time for foreign affairs. Because of war debts, reparations, etc., most Americans believed that their government should repossess the Prince of Wales. But they were too busy buying stocks and dancing the Black Bottom to give much attention to Congress's proposal that Europe be broken up for junk and sold to Japan.

The Bubble Bust
(*Sally Randicalism*)
XXIX

DRESSES WERE SELLING SHORT, BUT SO WERE THE STOCK brokers, so that the bottom fell out of the market.

Millions of Americans woke up one morning to find that they were ruined men. This was in addition to the usual number of ruined women. Many staggered out of their offices to dispatch themselves to the country "from whose bourn no traveller returns" (Argentina).

Others leapt from high buildings. In many firms seniority meant the right to jump first. Office boys, impatient, jumped from lower floors, thereby originating the American saying: "Be nice to people on your way up because you may meet them again on the way down."

The fall-out lasted several days, after which the country settled down for what was called the Depression,* or the Dirty Thirties, or the Golden Age of Bumming. President Hoover assured the country that prosperity was just around the corner, but his advisers were unable to locate the intersection.

* The Depression was the only period in American history when Americans have been broke without having to work for it.

Say, Uncle

A rumor that the banks were closing started a nationwide panic and run on the banks, which was eased only when the government promised to lend the banks a fiver till Friday.

The Golden Age of Railroading

A Wave of Initials XXX

THE PRESIDENT WHO STARTED THE NATION ON THE ROAD to recovery—or bankruptcy as it is better known to Republicans—was Franklin Delano Roosevelt. Roosevelt did this by issuing fireside chits, which the nation accepted in lieu of cash.

F.D.R. was also responsible for the NRA, the CCC, the AAA and many other modern aids to total confusion. He was the first American President to use the radio to sell himself and his party. For fifteen years the Republicans were known only as Brand X.

Roosevelt also tried to pack the Supreme Court, but it was full of old suits and refused to close, even when he sat on it.

XXXI World War Two and Over

MEANWHILE ADOLF HITLER, IN GERMANY, HAD BEEN doing his own version of the fireside chat by burning the Reichstag and raising his voice a little. This led to war, and the U.S. passed the Neutrality Act, which made it illegal for the American armed forces to fight over anything but a blonde.

But Japan attacked the U.S. anyhow, and soon the G.I.'s (named after their intrepid commander General Issue) were fighting on all fronts. They were inspired by Eisenhower, Bradley, and MacArthur at the front, and by Betty Grable from the rear. After Germany's surrender, the hardest struggles of the war were commemorated with the celebration of V.D. Day.

Harry the Atomizer XXXII

UNDER PRESIDENT TRUMAN THE UNITED STATES ENTERED the Atomic Age. The Atomic Age was '46 but looked about '80.

Atomic Fallout

The U.S. was now the country to which the entire world looked for guidance, preferably in the form of traveler's checks.

Say, Uncle

The invention of the atomic bomb was followed by development in the U.S. of an instrument of even more terrible power—television.

During the fifties the country became so prosperous that it could afford to forgive Mr. Hoover and concentrate on hating communism. Thanks to a Senator McCarthy, Washington, D.C., became the centre of a new mining industry engaged in digging up everybody's past.

Also in the fifties transportation changed dramatically, the jet aircraft revolutionizing air travel and Marilyn Monroe adding a new dimension to walking. A screen actress, Miss Monroe started her career by making the most important contribution to the calendar since Gregory XIII.

Politically the United States was under the Republicans, who made sure that its foreign policy ran in only the best circles.

All Americans agreed, however, that the country was in danger of being destroyed by an enemy within. They just couldn't decide whether this was communism or teenagers.

The Space Age, or Upsy Days XXXIII

THE ATOMIC AGE WAS SOON CROWDED INTO THE BACKground by the Space Age, not only in the Pentagon but in the rival service: comic books. When the Russians were the first to put a satellite into orbit around the earth, the President of the U.S. promised to use everything available to put an object into space—driver, brassie, No. 1 iron, or even a putter if necessary.

By 1960 the United States were confident that they could rocket a man into orbit, and soon after that land men on the moon, and—who knows?—they may find that new route to India.

AMERICA
TODAY

Freedom of Speech

THE FOUR

Freedom from Fear

Freedom of Worship

FREEDOMS

Freedom from Want

PAINTING IN AMERICA

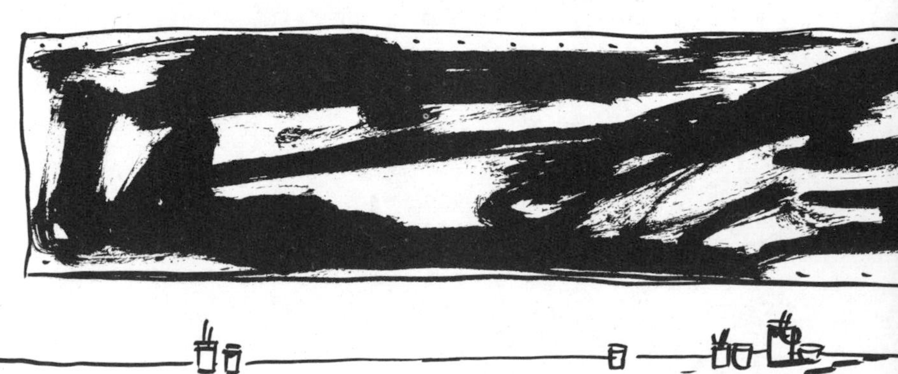

Economy Class

Vincent

Luxury Class

MUSIC

Tendency to Take Native Music Seriously

Delinquent (Juvenile)

see Business Illegit For Delinquent (Senior)

Business Legit

Business Illegit

Western (Juvenile)

Western (Authentic)

Western (Artistic)

Las Vegas Dress

Las Vegas Undress

California Functional

ARCHITECTURE

Southern Traditional

Rural Executive

Belief in Forgivene:

CHARACTER

Belief in the Democratic Way of Life

Belief in Youth

and Perpetual Youth

Tendency to Be a Good Sport

Belief in the Big Smile

Belief in the Family

Belief in Planned Obsolescence

Belief in Historic Traditions

Ability to Appreciate Natural Beauties

Appendix
(remove if rumbling)

A. American literature

The giants of American literature are Edgar Allan Poe, Thomas Wolfe and Dr. Spock. The first two are widely respected, though not read, whereas Dr. Spock has largely replaced grandmothers.

Since World War Two American novels can be divided into two classes: those that sell to only a small, select group of readers, and the dirty ones.

For a time some American novelists were held back from writing depraved novels not only by their own inherent sense of propriety but also by the difficulty in selling the movie rights. Recently, thanks to "adult" films, this last hurdle has been surmounted, and all best-selling authors are engaged in the literary equivalent of the Oklahoma Land Rush, each bent on staking his claim on the new frontier of abnormal sexual behavior. *Burgess Bedtime Stories* may have seen their last of Poor Mrs. Quack unless she turns out to be a nympho.

B. The U.S. and Canada

During the history of both these countries it has often been suggested that Canada and the U.S. should unite as one nation. The objection has been that when first cousins marry their issue is apt to be a breed of idiots.

A good example of the union of a small northern country with a larger neighbor to the south is that of Scotland and England. This marriage resulted in the spread of a particularly violent type of idiocy (golf).

It also led to the economic exploitation of one country by the other, the Bank of England being taken over by Scots who refused to let the English borrow their own money. The English became entirely dependent on Scotland for the necessities of life, namely whisky.

Another difficulty arises in Canada's becoming the fifty-first state, i.e., the fact that Canada is not only larger than Texas but larger than the entire United States (including Alaska). The addition of such a gigantic state to the Union could mean having to put Rhode Island under sedation.

Also, presidential candidates waging cross-country campaigns would have to travel twice as far, as would their wives, with a 100 per cent increase in fatigue and very possibly some ugly scenes on the back platform of the train.

SENATOR SLUGS SPOUSE IN STE. AGATHE is not the kind of newspaper headline Americans want to read.

The only feasible union of the two countries is therefore that of making the United States Canada's eleventh province.

In a single, masterful stroke the U.S. loses an identity

that is resented in many parts of the world and takes on the bland, inoffensive character that all countries know as Canada.

Americans will have a durable, high-test queen who is crowned regardless of how she looks in a bathing suit or whether she can play "Valse Triste" on the musical saw.

Best of all, the American people will once more be returned to the bosom of the British family of nations. The prodigal daughter, a little heavier, more buxom, will be back where she belongs, all of her brothers and sisters only too ready to forget that she ran away with that George fellow, and Mother England fondly patting the hand that wears those big, vulgar rocks.

This is our vision, dear reader. This is the soap opera *they didn't dare to write.*

This is the authors' dream. Some say that we have been carried away. Others say that if we haven't been we soon will be.

No matter. We have submitted this Grand Design for North American union to one of the most respected historians and scholars in the United States, and have been greatly stimulated by his reply, apart from its reference to "a snowball in Hell."

We feel that we have done our part. We now step back, and

(Ed. note: There was no footing.)